You Mad Because I'm Blessed?

Take it up with GOD!

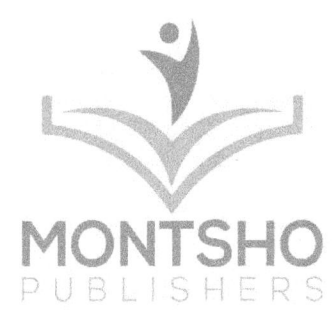

MONTSHO
PUBLISHERS

Montsho Publishers

Copyright 2019

ISBN 9781796536898

There is a Masterpiece in the Mind of Every Artist.

There is a Masterpiece in the Mind of Every Artist.

No great work of art is ever finished.

No great work of art is ever finished.

In order to show the light you need the dark.

Always draw it just the way you see it. Don't worry about how you 'should' draw it.

Always draw it just the way you see it. Don't worry about how you 'should' draw it.

The seed of your next artwork lies embedded in the imperfections of your current piece.

The seed of your next artwork lies embedded in the imperfections of your current piece.

Creativity happens when you leave your comfort zone

The residue of time wasted is Creativity.

Expressing yourself artistically is the only way to run away without leaving home.

Painting is just another way of keeping a diary.

Painting is just another way of keeping a diary.

There is no must in art because art is free.

There is no must in art because art is free.

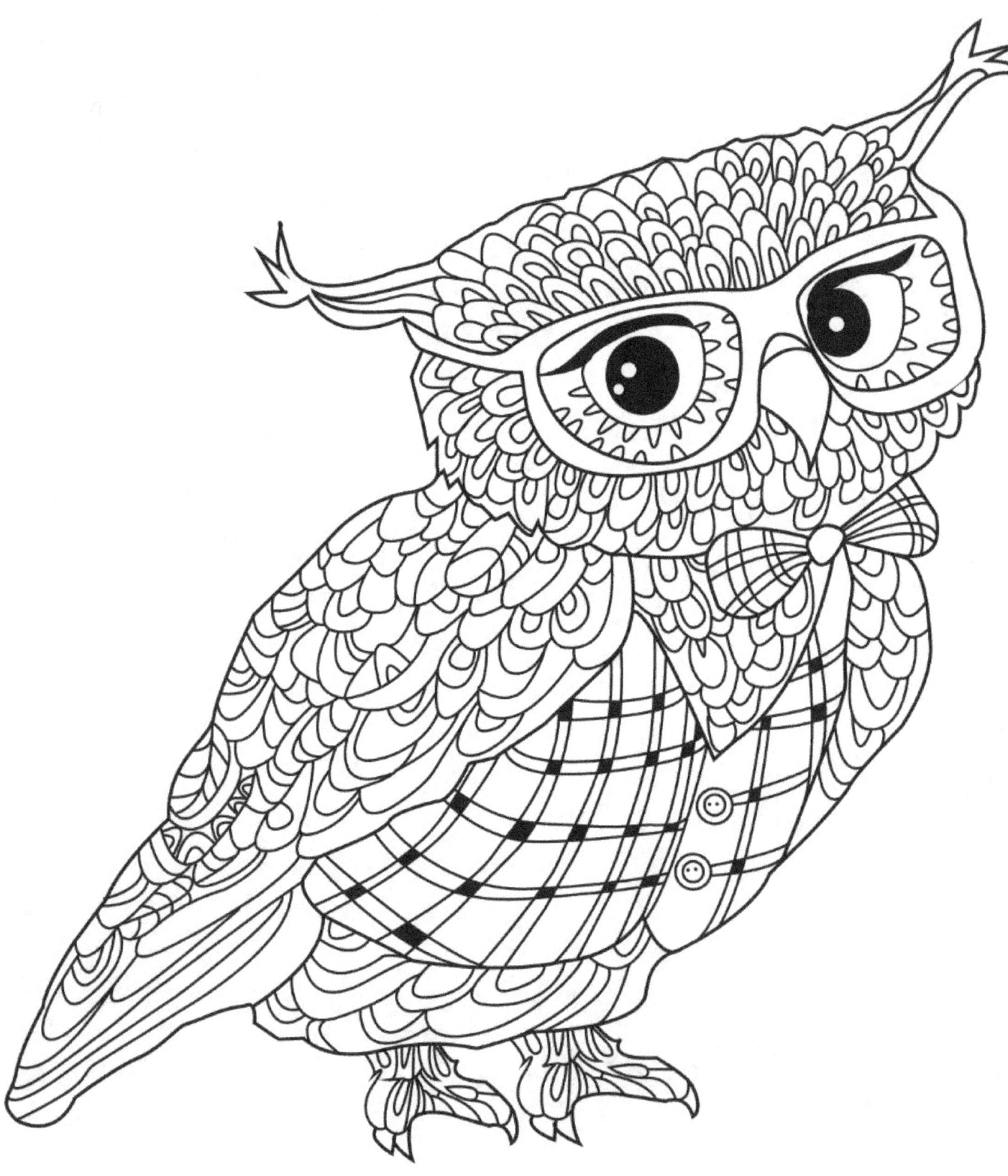

The day an Artist dares not to please, is the day he discovers his genius.

The purpose of art is washing the dust of daily life off our souls.

Art is the expression of the soul living its best life.

Art is the expression of the soul living its best life.

If you are ever fearful to display your art, then you have created what the world needs to see.

If you are ever fearful to display your art, then you have created what the world needs to see.

The function of an Artist is to affirm and glorify life.

The function of an Artist is to affirm and glorify life.

Art is a way to escape from reality.

Art is a way to escape from reality.

The aim of art is to represent not the outward appearance of things,

but their inward significance.

Art is life and belongs to everybody, you're just the genius that brings it.

A simple line painted with the brush can lead to freedom and happiness.

The meaning of life is to find your gift. The purpose of life is to give it away.

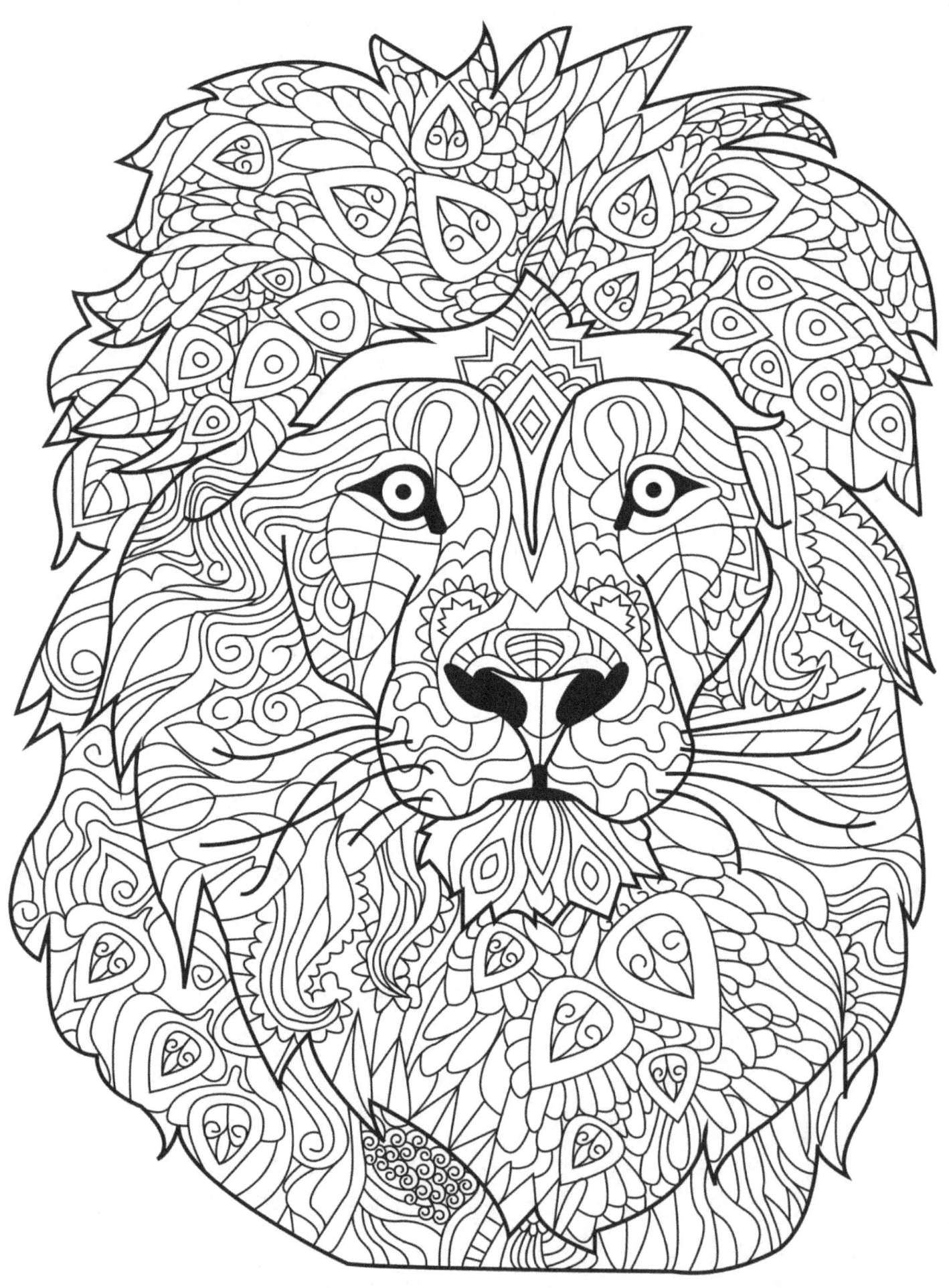

Life is more important than art; that's what makes art important.

Spirit and art are intertwined.

One must work and dare if one really wants to live.

I am not sick. I am broken. But I am happy to be alive as long as I can paint.

A work of art which did not begin in emotion is not art.

A work of art which did not begin in emotion is not art.

Art must be an expression of love or it is nothing.

Nothing can be accomplished without love.

If you don't create from the heart, your work will always be lacking.

If you don't create from the heart, your work will always be lacking.

I would rather die of passion than of boredom.

I would rather die of passion than of boredom.

I feel that there is nothing more truly artistic than to love people.

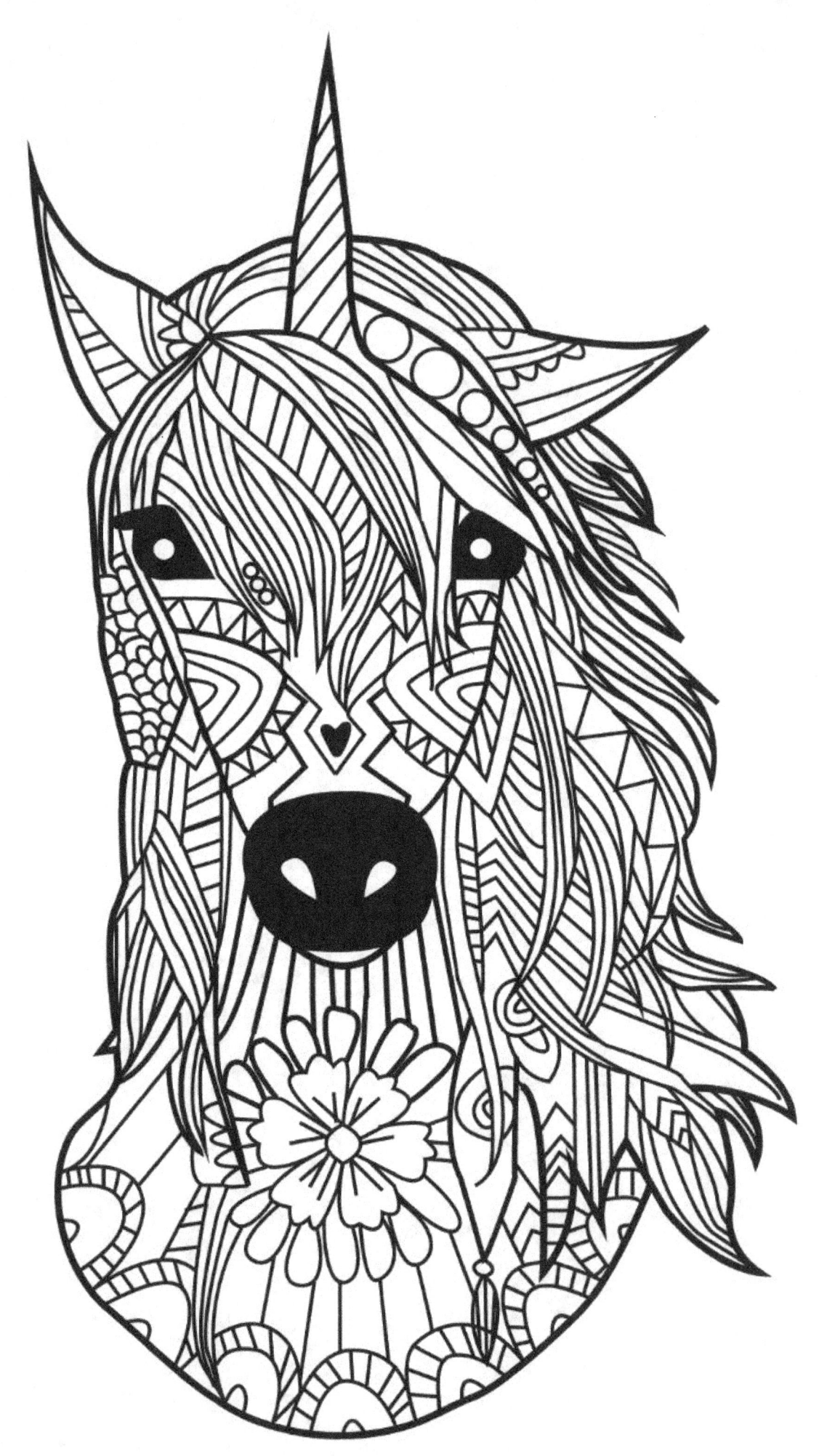

A masterpiece is inevitable when love and skill work together.

A masterpiece is inevitable when love and skill work together.

An artist is paid for his vision not his labor.

An artist is paid for his vision not his labor.

Art is not what you see, but what you make others see.

I use my paintbrush to say what I can't put into words.

Art is the most intense mode of individualism that the world has known.

It is better to paint from memory, for thus your work will be your own.

It is better to paint from memory, for thus your work will be your own.

It is better to fail in originality than to succeed in imitation.

I don't paint things. I only paint the difference between things.

I don't paint things. I only paint the difference between things.

The thermometer of success is merely the jealousy of the haters.

The thermometer of success is merely the jealousy of the haters.

The artist must train not only his eye but also his soul.

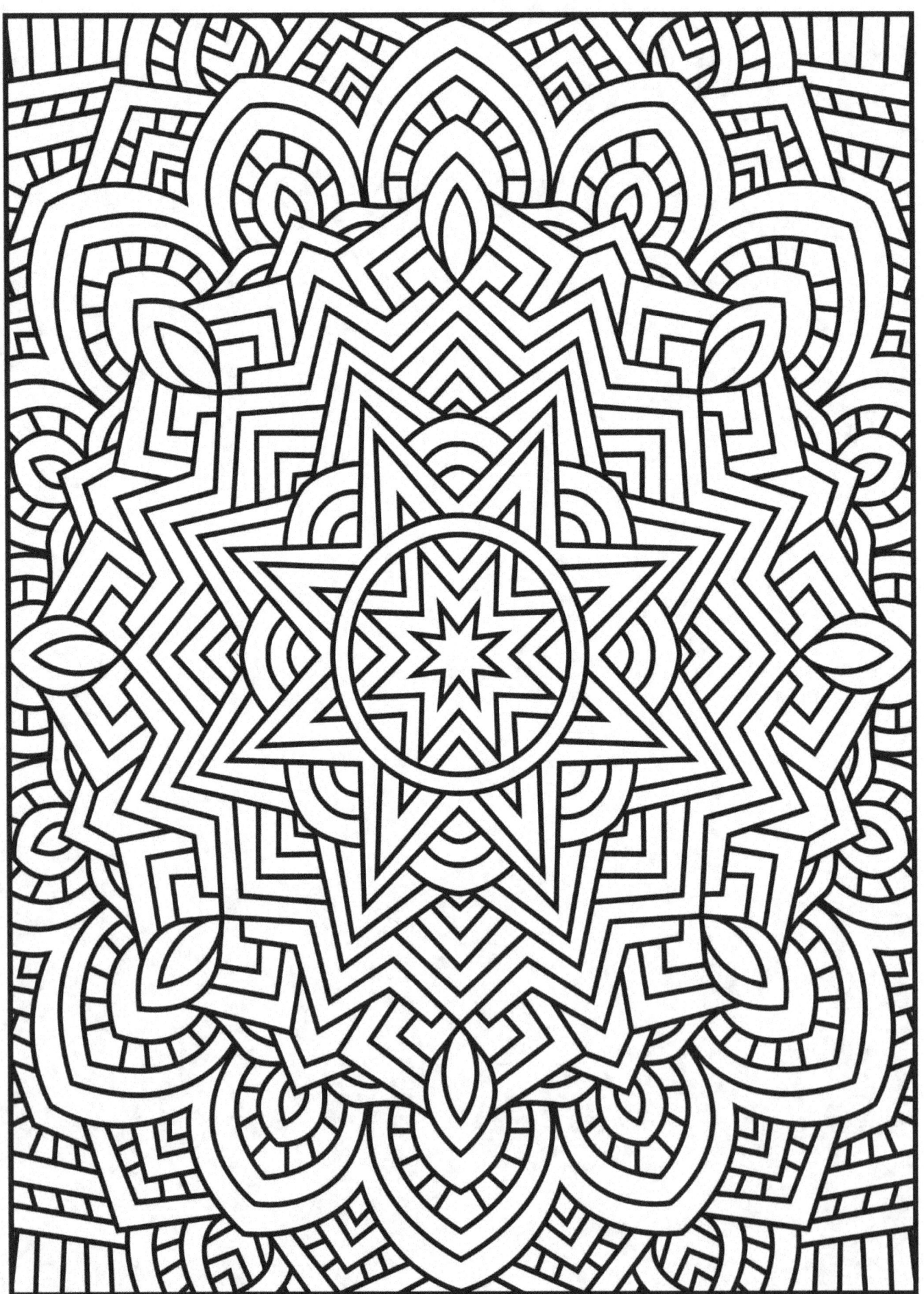

All the time you waste trying to be better than others should be used on your craft instead.

Creativity is the expression of one's uniqueness.

Creativity is the expression of one's uniqueness.

There is no abstract art. You must always start with something.

Afterward you can remove all traces of reality.

Every line is the actual experience with its own unique story.

My painting feels like a pianist tickling the ivories.

My painting feels like a pianist tickling the ivories.

One person's craziness is another person's reality.

One person's craziness is another person's reality.

Art has always treaded the line of revolution and plagiarism.

Art has always treaded the line of revolution and plagiarism.

Don't let common sense stifle your creativity.

You can't fail as an Artist. Being an Artist is a success in its own right.

You can't fail as an Artist. Being an Artist is a success in its own right.

Art is meant to disturb, science reassures the disturbance.

Art is meant to disturb, science reassures the disturbance.

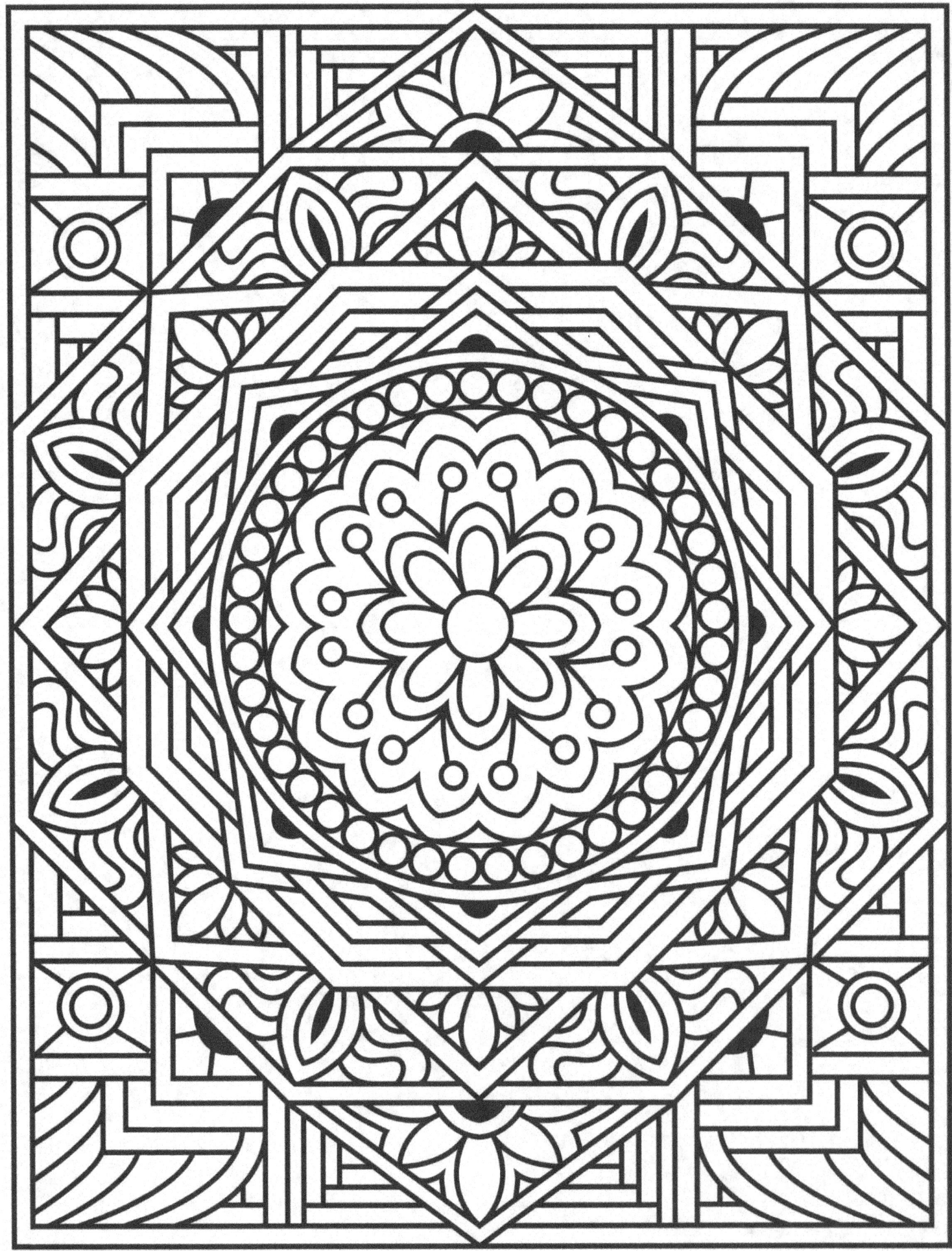

My Art speaks for itself.

My Art speaks for itself.

An artist should never be a prisoner of himself, prisoner of style, prisoner of reputation, prisoner of success.

The best reason to paint is that there is no reason to paint.

The best reason to paint is that there is no reason to paint.

A masterpiece is inevitable when love and skill work together.

An artist is paid for his vision not his labor.

An artist is paid for his vision not his labor.

As an Artist your skill is what you make people see, feel, and hear.

As an Artist your skill is what you make people see, feel, and hear.

I use my paintbrush to say what I can't put into words.

I use my paintbrush to say what I can't put into words.

Individualism is Art at its best.

To ensure your work is your own, always paint from memory.

It is better to fail in originality than to succeed in imitation.

Plagiarism is the lack of creativity.

Plagiarism is the lack of creativity.

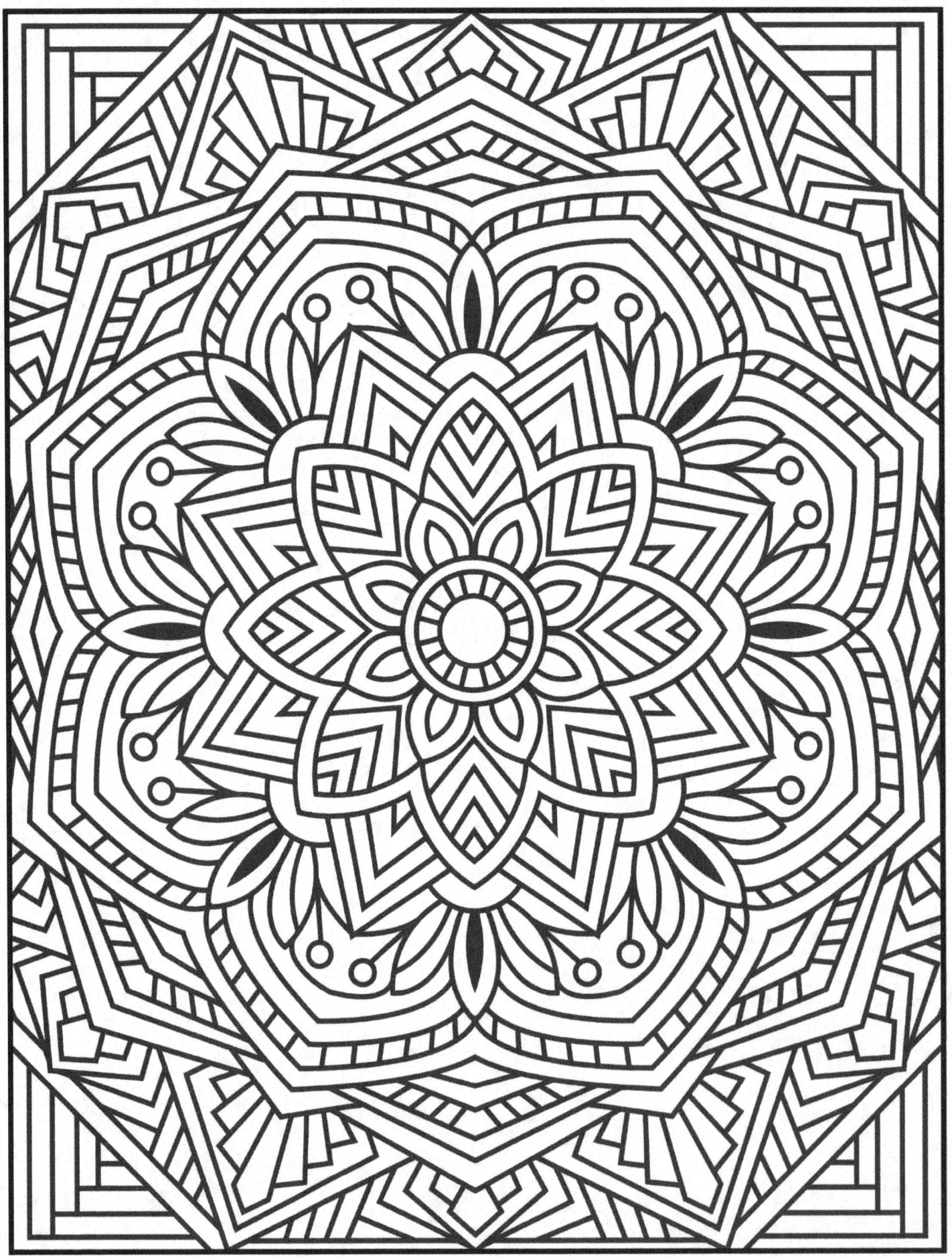

There is a Masterpiece in the Mind of Every Artist.

No great work of art is ever finished.

No great work of art is ever finished.

In order to show the light you need the dark.

In order to show the light you need the dark.

Don't worry about how you 'should' draw it. Just draw it the way you see it.

Don't worry about how you 'should' draw it. Just draw it the way you see it.

The seed of your next artwork lies embedded in the imperfections of your current piece.

The seed of your next artwork lies embedded in the imperfections of your current piece.

Creativity happens when you leave your comfort zone.

There is no such thing as extra time, creativity should always be at work.

There is no such thing as extra time, creativity should always be at work.

Art is the only way to run away without leaving home.

Art is the only way to run away without leaving home.

Painting is just another way of keeping a diary.

Painting is just another way of keeping a diary.

There is no must in art because art is free.

There is no must in art because art is free.

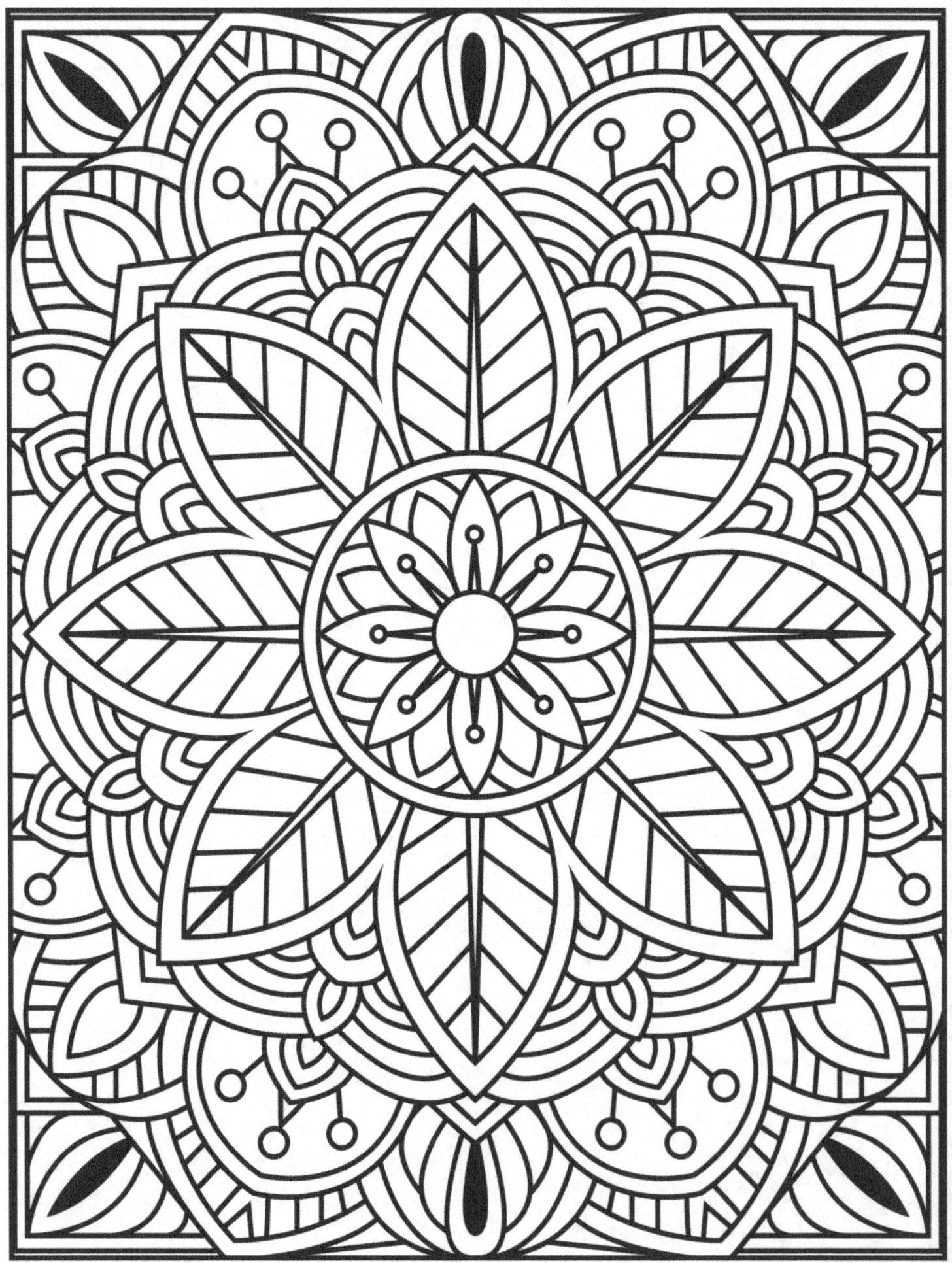

An artist discovers his genius the day he dares not to please.

When you free your mind the creativity begins.

When you free your mind the creativity begins.

Art is the expression of the soul living its best life.

Art is the expression of the soul living its best life.

Art should comfort the disturbed and disturb the comfortable.

.

Art should comfort the disturbed and disturb the comfortable.

The function of an Artist is to affirm and glorify life.

The function of an Artist is to affirm and glorify life.

Art is an escape from reality.

Art is an escape from reality.

The aim of art is to represent not the outward appearance of things,

but their inward significance.

The aim of art is to represent not the outward appearance of things,

but their inward significance.

Art is life and belongs to everybody, you're just the genius that brings it.

Art is life and belongs to everybody, you're just the genius that brings it.

A simple line painted with the brush can lead to freedom and happiness.

The meaning of life is to find your gift. The purpose of life is to give it away.

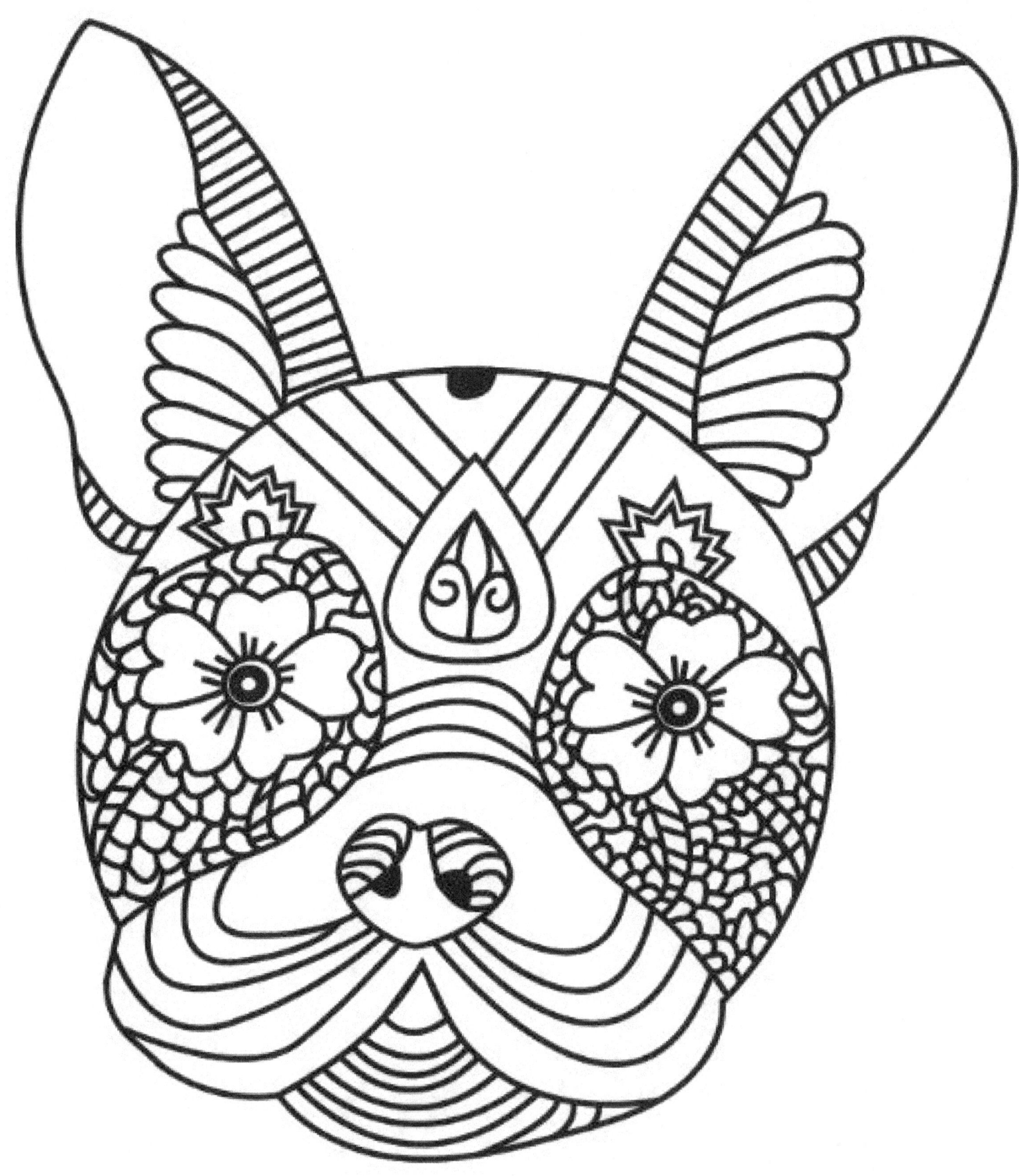

Life is more important than art; that's what makes art important.

Spirit and art are intertwined.

Spirit and art are intertwined.

To live freely you must push the boundaries of acceptance.

I am not sick. I am broken. But I am happy to be alive as long as I can paint.

A work of art which did not begin in emotion is not art.

A work of art which did not begin in emotion is not art.

Art must be an expression of love or it is nothing.

Art must be an expression of love or it is nothing.

Nothing can be accomplished without love.

If you don't create from the heart, your work will always be lacking.

If you don't create from the heart, your work will always be lacking.

I would rather die of passion than of boredom.

I would rather die of passion than of boredom.

I feel that there is nothing more truly artistic than to love people.

I feel that there is nothing more truly artistic than to love people.

I don't paint things. I only paint the difference between things.

I don't paint things. I only paint the difference between things.

The thermometer of success is merely the jealousy of the haters.

The thermometer of success is merely the jealousy of the haters.

The residue of time wasted is Creativity.

The residue of time wasted is Creativity.

No great work of art is ever finished.

No great work of art is ever finished.

www.ingramcontent.com/pod-product-compliance
Lightning Source LLC
Chambersburg PA
CBHW081721220526

45468CB00008B/1928